A Guide for Using

My Side of the Mountain

in the Classroom

Based on the book written by
Jean Craighead George

*This guide written by **Debra J. Housel, M.S. Ed.***

Teacher Created Materials, Inc.
6421 Industry Way
Westminster, CA 92683
www.teachercreated.com
©*2001 Teacher Created Materials, Inc.*
Reprinted, 2003
Made in U.S.A.
ISBN-0-7439-3061-4

Illustrated by
Ben De Soto

Edited by
Gisela Lee

Cover Art by
Bruce Hedges

Table of Contents

Introduction

One of the most enjoyable things about teaching is using a book as stimulating and entertaining as *My Side of the Mountain*. From the book's opening line, Jean Craighead George encourages readers to experience wilderness survival through an independent, resourceful teenage boy named Sam Gribley.

My Side of the Mountain provides many opportunities for students to discuss wildlife, wilderness survival, and the importance of nonfiction reading. Not only will this literature unit entertain, it will provide a wealth of teachable moments. The features of this literature unit are listed below.

- A Sample Lesson Plan

- Pre-reading Activities

- Biographical Information and Sketch of the Author

- A Book Summary

- Vocabulary Lists by Section

- Vocabulary Activity Ideas

- Chapters of the book grouped by sections, each of which include:
    - *quizzes*
    - *hands-on projects*
    - *cooperative learning opportunities*
    - *cross-curricular activities*
    - *connections to relate to the reader's own life*

- Post-reading Activities, including book report ideas

- Culminating Activities

- Three Different Options for Unit Tests:
    - *Objective (Matching and True/False/Explain)*
    - *Explaining Quotes From the Book (Chapters are indicated in case you want the students to reread the context prior to responding.)*
    - *Conversations (Students write conversation scripts for characters)*

- A Bibliography and Related Resources

- Answer Key

This literature unit will be an invaluable addition to your literature planning. By using these ideas, your students will discover the delightful companionship to be found in a good book.

Sample Lesson Plan

Each of the lessons suggested below can take between one and three days to complete. Adapt the lesson if you feel it will be beneficial for the needs of your students.

Lesson 1

- Complete some or all of the pre-reading activities (page 5).
- Read About the Author to your students (page 6).
- Read the book's preface aloud to the class.
- Introduce the vocabulary for section 1 (page 8).
- Choose a vocabulary activity (page 9).
- Read chapters 1–3.

Lesson 2

- Discuss chapters 1–3.
- Do Quiz Time for section 1 (page 10).
- Begin Reader's Response Journal (page 16).
- Play Brown Bag Mystery Game (page 11).
- Form literature circles (page 12).
- Learn about the animal kingdom (pages 13–15).
- Conduct research in the library (page 23).
- Introduce vocabulary for section 2 (page 8).
- Read chapters 4–9.

Lesson 3

- Discuss chapters 4–9.
- Do Quiz Time for section 2 (page 17).
- Write a journal entry for chapters 4–9.
- Design a mobile (page 18).
- Identify causes and their effects (pages 19 and 20).
- Learn about the plant and fungi kingdoms (pages 21 and 22).
- Introduce vocabulary for section 3 (page 8).
- Choose a vocabulary activity (page 9).
- Read chapters 10–12.

Lesson 4

- Discuss chapters 10–12.
- Do Quiz Time for section 3 (page 24).
- Write a journal entry for chapters 10–12.
- Build Sam's mountain (page 25).
- Form "expert" teams (page 26).

- Write in the active voice (page 27).
- Research your family tree (page 28).
- Introduce vocabulary for section 4 (page 8).
- Read chapters 13–16.
- Choose a vocabulary activity (page 9).

Lesson 5

- Discuss chapters 13–16.
- Do Quiz Time for section 4 (page 29).
- Write a journal entry for chapters 13–16.
- Make a model of Sam's tree house (page 30).
- Play Stump the Experts (page 31).
- Complete Math Word Problems (page 32).
- Invent portmanteau words (page 33).
- Introduce vocabulary for section 5 (page 8).
- Read chapters 17–22.
- Choose a vocabulary activity (page 9).

Lesson 6

- Discuss chapters 17–22.
- Do Quiz Time for section 5 (page 34).
- Write a journal entry for chapters 17–22.
- Assemble a jackdaw (page 35).
- Do Creative Review Questions (page 36).
- Recognize figurative language (page 37).
- Compare Yourself to Sam (page 38).
- Begin a culminating activity (page 40).

Lesson 7

- Watch the videotape version of *My Side of the Mountain* (listed on page 39).
- Discuss the videotape.
- Assign book report (page 39).
- Complete a culminating activity (page 40).

Lesson 8

- Choose one or more test formats to evaluate students (pages 41–43).
- Discuss test responses.
- Discuss the students' enjoyment of the book.
- Provide a list of related reading for your students (pages 44 and 45).

Before the Book

Before you read *My Side of the Mountain* with your students, do some pre-reading activities to stimulate the students' interest and enhance their comprehension. Here are some activities and discussion questions for use with your class.

1. Ask the students to look at the book's cover and predict what the story will be about. Record these predictions on butcher paper and keep them posted throughout the unit. Have the students refer to their predictions occasionally throughout the literature unit to compare their pre-reading ideas to what actually happens in the story.

2. Brainstorm on a piece of chart paper any information the students know about wilderness survival.

3. Read the book's preface aloud to the class, stopping to discuss the meaning of the following words: *dissuade, foraging, saplings, sentinel,* and *naturalist.*

4. Ask for volunteers to recount their own "running away" adventures.

5. Examine the novel's key themes: running away and independence. Have the students speculate about the following questions either in a class discussion or through journal entries.

   • What factors could prompt a teen to run away to the wilderness?

   • Why would a teen be willing to leave behind friends and family?

   • What conditions at home might encourage someone to run away?

   • When the odds are against you to succeed at something, what character qualities does it take to succeed?

   • What are the problems a teenager trying to survive in the wilderness might face?

   • Why would a teen be willing to face these risks?

6. Ask the students about other books by Jean Craighead George that they may have read.

7. Ask the students if any of them have ever trained a pet and to tell about some of their experiences during training.

8. Discuss with the students ways for them to identify the setting (especially with regards to time). Some may feel that the story is contemporary. Most people believe it takes place during the 1930s or 1940s (before school attendance became compulsory, when hitchhiking and picking up hitchhikers was common, and wooded mountains were not under aerial fire watch surveillance, etc.). Jean Craighead George never defines the time, so it is up to the readers to decide when the story takes place. (The students will be asked to justify their decision in the first quiz.)

About the Author

For over 50 years, Jean Craighead George has sparked a love of nature in young people as both a writer and illustrator of fiction and nonfiction books. Born on July 2, 1919, in Washington, D.C., to a father who was a naturalist, she became fascinated with all aspects of nature at an early age. As the younger sister of twin brothers, she followed them everywhere, developing a reputation as a tomboy in the process. Her brothers taught her how to fish, catch frogs, play softball, and eventually spelunk. She attended Pennsylvania State University, receiving her bachelor's degree in 1941.

Jean married John George in January 1944 after a brief four-month courtship. During his tour of duty with the navy during World War II, the couple spent a lot of time apart. To compensate, they decided to write books together. As a result, their first book was published in 1948, and they went on to co-author another five. Their marriage produced a daughter and two sons before it ended in divorce in early 1963.

Published in 1959, *My Side of the Mountain* was the third book Jean wrote independently. It immediately received Newbery honor status and later earned the George G. Stone Center for Children's Books award. The book appeals to young readers because Sam Gribley, like all of Jean's protagonists, is a child "searching for independence and self-knowledge." Her literary style also makes ecological systems and scientific research both interesting and relevant. Since she needs to know many fine details to write such realistic fiction, Jean has always conducted extensive field research prior to writing any book. For example, before creating her Newbery award-winning book, *Julie of the Wolves*, she traveled to Alaska to spend a great deal of time talking with Inuit Native Americans and studying wolves.

In 1968 Jean received the honor of Woman of the Year from her alma mater, Pennsylvania State University. Today Jean makes her home in Chappaqua, New York, with a parrot named Tocca and an Alaskan malamute dog called Qimmiq. Some of her many interests include writing (of course), painting nature scenes, visiting colleges and laboratories of natural science, and white water canoeing.

My Side of the Mountain

by Jean Craighead George
(*1960 Newbery Honor Book*)

*Available from E. P. Dutton, 1988 (school and library binding); Penguin USA, 1988
(hardcover); Viking Press, 1991 (paperback); VHS video, rated G, 1969*

As the oldest of nine children, Sam Gribley longs for a more peaceful life far away from his family's cramped New York City apartment. He begins reading about wilderness survival and eventually fulfills his dreams by running away to his great-grandfather's abandoned land near Delhi, New York, in the Catskill Mountains. *My Side of the Mountain* details Sam's many adventures as he struggles to co-exist with nature by living inside a hollow tree on the mountainside for an entire year.

When he first arrives in the spring, Sam doesn't even know exactly where the Gribley land is located and must go to the nearest public library to research the matter. During his first evening alone, Sam has difficulty starting a fire and spends a wretched night cold and wet. The next day he meets a kind man who teaches him how to start a fire with flint and steel. From that moment on, Sam knows he can conquer the mountain. He learns to make and bait traps, watches what the animals eat to locate edible wild plants and roots, and burns out the interior of a massive tree to create a cozy, yet inconspicuous, dwelling.

Sam has companionship in the form of a female falcon named Frightful. After risking his life to snatch Frightful from her mother's nest, he trains her to hunt small game for him. Together, he and Frightful make a powerful hunting team, assuring Sam of a continual food supply even in the dead of winter. He also develops an unusual friendship with a weasel whom he nicknames The Baron.

Several times Sam walks to the local library where the librarian, Miss Turner, agrees to keep his whereabouts a secret. She helps him research how to train his falcon and even gives him a haircut to help him look less conspicuous.

Throughout Sam's time away, rumors fly that a "wild boy" is hiding somewhere on the mountain. To avoid being sent back to the drudgery of civilization, Sam has to evade the fire warden that comes looking for him, an elderly town resident who insists he help her pick strawberries, and many hikers and hunters. Sam meets a college professor whom he affectionately calls Bando who stays with him for several weeks, and he doesn't let Sam's secret slip.

At Christmas Sam's father comes looking for him and is delighted by the tree home and store of provisions Sam has accumulated. He agrees to allow Sam to stay through the winter. Winter brings new challenges in the form of freezing temperatures, a blizzard, and an ice storm. In the spring, a young newspaper reporter discovers Sam and "tells all," essentially destroying his lifestyle. Just then his entire family shows up, announcing they've come to live with him on the mountain (but in a "proper" house).

In 1969, *My Side of the Mountain* was adapted as a film by Paramount Pictures.

Vocabulary Lists

Section 1
(Chapters 1–3)

blizzard	tethers	venture	upholstered	gangplank
conquer	ravines	cascades	penknife	combustible
emphatic	misstep	boundary	congregate	notches
whiskery	lolled	foundation	subscriptions	whittle
trenches	folly	tinder	flint and steel	venison
riffles	eddies	charred	boughs	

Section 2
(Chapter 4–9)

nourishing	remote	coltish	teetered	saucy
smoldering	nonedible	implements	starchy	botanical
skittered	talons	bristles	flanges	dappled
citified	savory	corm	wiry	pinfeathers
shinnied	acrid	snare	rumpus	quiver (both
primitive	dales	exertion	warden	meanings)

Section 3
(Chapter 10–12)

tarry	provoke	backwatering	vengeance	tannic acid
furtively	reassured	scuttled	tedious	Desdemondia
carcass	lure	quartered	preened	membrane
hysterics	abundance	maneuvers	chittering	marksmanship
ferocious	evidently	racketeer	fragrant	personable
Thoreau	winced	poaching	underworld	close-cropped

Section 4
(Chapters 13–16)

ashcans	shaft	cavot	cache	precaution
devour	verge	plumage	tallow	indignity
sputter	ferocity	ventilate	complaint	utterly
drenched	wavery	superb	gorge	nerve-racking

Section 5
(Chapters 17–22)

quarry	flashbulb	resort	sensationalism	bole
originated	adorned	undercoverts	bearing	fatigue
bleakness	serenade	conservationists	ingenuity	barometer
wistfully	rendition	insulating	sanguine	concoction
sired	outwit	crag	copse	hammocks
humanity	untoward	probability	forum	hordes
momentum	editorials	inferring	resounding	

Vocabulary Activity Ideas

Help your students learn and retain the vocabulary in *My Side of the Mountain* by providing them with interesting activities such as these.

❑ **Word Searches and Crossword Puzzles**

Word searches and crossword puzzles are fun for all ages. Students can use the vocabulary words from the story to create puzzles individually or in teams. Have them exchange papers and solve one another's puzzles. When the papers are completed, the authors can correct them.

❑ **Vocabulary Spelling Words**

Encourage the usage of vocabulary words by using them as your weekly spelling words. Writing sentences or paragraphs is also an effective way to expand usage.

❑ **Television Show**

A television news broadcast is a great way to give the students further experiences in using vocabulary words. Put the students into groups of no more than four students. Assign each student a job in the "studio": anchor, co-anchor, producers, and meteorologist. Have them use the vocabulary words in a contest. Have each team present a broadcast to the class. As they present, use a vocabulary list for each group and check off each word as they use it. Award a prize to the group that uses the greatest number of vocabulary words.

❑ **Vocabulary Treasure Hunt**

Have a vocabulary treasure hunt. You can do this individually or in small groups. The idea is for the students to find and cut out as many of the vocabulary words as possible. Encourage them to search magazines, newspapers, printed advertisements, etc. They should mount each word they find on a 3" x 5" (8 cm x 13 cm) card and write its definition. If a student finds a word in a place that cannot be cut out (i.e., a book or billboard), have him or her write the word and where he or she saw it on the card along with the definition. The student who wins is the one who finds the most words. This is a powerful technique for making your students more aware of and alert to new vocabulary words.

❑ **Vocabulary Cartoon Strip**

Create vocabulary cartoon strips using 24" x 6" (61 cm x 15 cm) strips of poster paper. Have the students fold their strips in half, then in half again, and then in half once more to make eight cartoon windows per strip. Challenge the students to use eight vocabulary words in their cartoon strips. Depending on your students' skill level, this could be done individually or in groups.

❑ **Vocabulary Word Synonyms**

Find and copy the sentence in which the word occurs in the book. Underline the word, and then write a synonym or synonymous phrase next to the underlined word. For an even greater challenge, have the students find and copy the sentence in which the word occurs in the book, underline the word, and then write an antonym or antonymous phrase next to the underlined word. This activity will also provide valuable practice in using a thesaurus.

❑ **Vocabulary Bingo Game**

Play a class vocabulary bingo game. Give each student a blank bingo grid. Have students write one vocabulary word in each space on the grid. Students may place the words in any order. Then you act as the caller, randomly choosing and reading the vocabulary definitions. (Be sure you write down the words for which you've read the definitions so that you can verify a winning card.) Students place markers (beans, beads, pieces of paper, etc.) over the words that match the definitions read. A student wins by covering a row, column, or diagonal of words.

Quiz Time

Teacher Note: *Each quiz question indicates which level of Bloom's taxonomy it addresses: K = knowledge, C = comprehension, AP = application, AN = analysis, S = synthesis, and E = evaluation.*

Directions: Read each question carefully and answer on the lines provided.

1. What is the setting (time and place) of this story? (K) _____

   _____

2. Why does Sam run away to the Catskill Mountains? (C) _____

   _____

3. From what you've already learned about Sam Gribley, what are two of his personality traits? (AP)

   _____

   _____

4. Contrast Sam's feelings before and after the big snowstorm. (AN) _____

   _____

5. Discuss at least two problems Sam has during his first night on his own. (S) _____

   _____

   _____

6. Do you agree with Sam's statement that once he can catch fish and make fire he can conquer the Catskills? Explain why. (E) _____

   _____

   _____

7. Who is The Baron? (K) _____

   _____

8. Describe how Sam locates the Gribley farm. (C) _____

   _____

9. Name at least two obstacles that could have prevented Sam's plan to "live off the land" from working. (AP) _____

   _____

10. Who are the two people who are the most helpful in getting Sam started on his venture? How did they help? (AN) _____

    _____

11. Why do you think Sam has a trained falcon? (S) _____

    _____

12. Do you think it was a good idea for Sam to leave New York City to live inside a tree on a mountain? Explain why or why not. (E) _____

    _____

Brown Bag Mystery Game

Materials

- paper lunch bag for each student
- 3" x 5" (8 cm x 13 cm) card for each student

Directions

1. Ask each student to bring from home one small object that has something to do with the outdoors, wilderness survival, or events that have already occurred in *My Side of the Mountain*.
2. Pass out a paper bag to each student. Ask each student to put his or her object into the bag.
3. Stress to the students that their objects are not to be discussed or shown to anyone else prior to the game.
4. Each student should write a brief description of the object in the bag on a 3" x 5" (8 cm x 13 cm) card. Encourage each student to be creative and enigmatic in this description so as not to give away the item's identity.

Game Rules (tell the students at the outset of the game)

1. If teammates shout out guesses, the team forfeits its turn and play reverts to the other team.
2. Synonyms must be accepted. (For example, flower for dandelion.)
3. The person who is guessing should not be allowed to hold, feel, or in any way touch the bag.

Playing the Game

1. Divide the class into two teams.
2. Have a student from Team 1 stand in front of the class holding his or her bag and 3" x 5" (8 cm x 13 cm) card. A student from Team 2 comes up, reads the description aloud, and makes a guess about what's in the bag.
3. If the player guesses correctly, the object is shown and Team 2 gets a point.
4. If the player guesses incorrectly, a player from Team 1 comes up, reads the description aloud, and makes a guess about what's in the bag.
5. If the player guesses correctly, the object is shown and Team 1 gets a point.
6. If the player guesses incorrectly, a new player from Team 2 comes up and repeats the process.
7. Play continues until someone guesses correctly what is in each student's bag. The team with the most points wins.

Some Item Ideas (Only share a few of these with your students and only if they're at a loss as to how to complete the assignment.)

tree bark	leaf	feather	grass	cattail head
twig	blueberry jam	chestnut	flint and steel	stone

After the Game

- Discuss the clue words in the descriptions that helped the listeners figure out the item's identity.
- Discuss how each item has already been used or how it may be used later in the story.
- For a challenging critical thinking activity, divide the students into groups of three. Ask the group members to remove the items from their bags and try to identify every characteristic that their items have in common (e.g., all found outdoors, all made of molecules, etc.).

Literature Circles

Discuss the importance of titles, first lines, and last lines. Talented authors like Jean Craighead George choose their titles carefully to make a connection between the title and the text. Although some stories begin with "Once upon a time," most authors use the opening line of a story to immediately set the tone and grab the reader's interest. Good last lines of books not only leave the reader with a sense of closure but also encourage the reader to reflect upon the book. George pulls the reader into the book with an intriguing opening, and her ending leaves the reader hoping for a sequel (of which there are two in the case of *My Side of the Mountain*).

The following activity will make students aware of the importance of titles, first lines, and last lines. This activity can improve students' own creative writing pieces, encouraging them to create interesting titles, first lines, and last lines.

Materials

- Have each student of the group bring in one book for this lesson (preferably his or her favorite story).
- three pieces of construction paper or sentence strips for each group
- marking pens

Directions

1. With the entire class, read and discuss the first line, last line, and title of *My Side of the Mountain*. How did the author use her first line to entice you to read more? Since you have not yet finished the book, what do you think of the last line? How does it make you feel? What importance does the title have to the story? Why do you think George chose *My Side of the Mountain* as the title?

2. Divide the students into literature circles of four. Each member should share his or her favorite book. While sharing, each student must read the book's title, first line, and last line, and tell why it's his or her favorite book.

3. After everyone in the group has shared, the group members should select their favorite first line, last line, and title among the four books. (These do not have to be from the same book, although they can be.) On the construction paper or sentence strips, write the favorite first line, last line, and title separately.

4. Reconvene as a whole group after first assembling all the first lines, last lines, and titles in categories on a board where everyone can see them. Request that a group member from each literature circle share the group's selections. You can also vote as a whole class for the overall favorite first line, last line, and title.

5. Conclude with a class discussion of the following points:
   - What do these lines have in common?
   - Are there some that stand out? In what way?
   - How do they catch a reader's interest?
   - What do you like about them?
   - What makes a book's title "catchy"?
   - Must a book title have significance to the rest of the book? In what way?

Animal Classification

Preparation

1. Prepare the graphic organizers on the next two pages on butcher paper without the information filled in and place them on a bulletin board or wall where all the students can see them.

2. Teach a lesson about the classifications and divisions of the animal kingdom as you discuss and fill in the graphic organizers with the class.

3. Have the students copy the graphic organizers and information into their notes.

4. Then have the students do the activity outlined below.

Materials

- poster board or tagboard
- 52 blank 3" x 5" (8 cm x 13 cm) cards
- fishing line or string
- scissors
- glue

Directions

1. Using the information provided on the graphic organizers on pages 14 and 15, write one animal's name on each of the blank cards prior to beginning this activity.

2. Divide the students into groups of four.

3. Assign each group one of the animal kingdom groups (mammals, arthropods, etc.).

4. The students need to draw and cut from the poster board this animal group's name using letters that are about 18 inches (46 cm) high.

5. Hang the names from the ceiling with the fishing line or string. If necessary, place them on a bulletin board or a wall.

6. Randomly distribute the cards with the animal names to the class members.

7. Ask the students to glue the cards onto the letters in the group name to which the animal belongs. They will probably need to trim the card to fit or to go around the curve of the letters.

8. If a student does not know what group his or her animal belongs to, he or she may discuss it with the group members or look up the animal in a dictionary or encyclopedia.

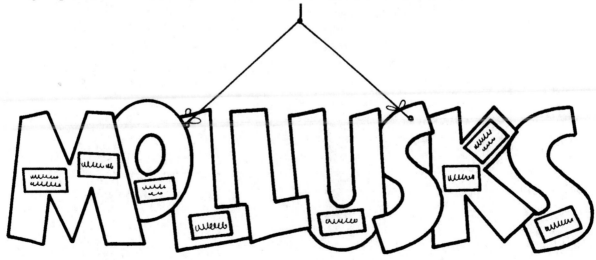

Animal Kingdom

all breathe, reproduce, use senses, eat plants and/or other animals, and usually can move their body

Vertebrates

Vertebrates have a backbone and a skeleton which holds the body together. Many have skulls to protect their complex brains; usually they have two or four limbs and a jaw to grab or chew food.

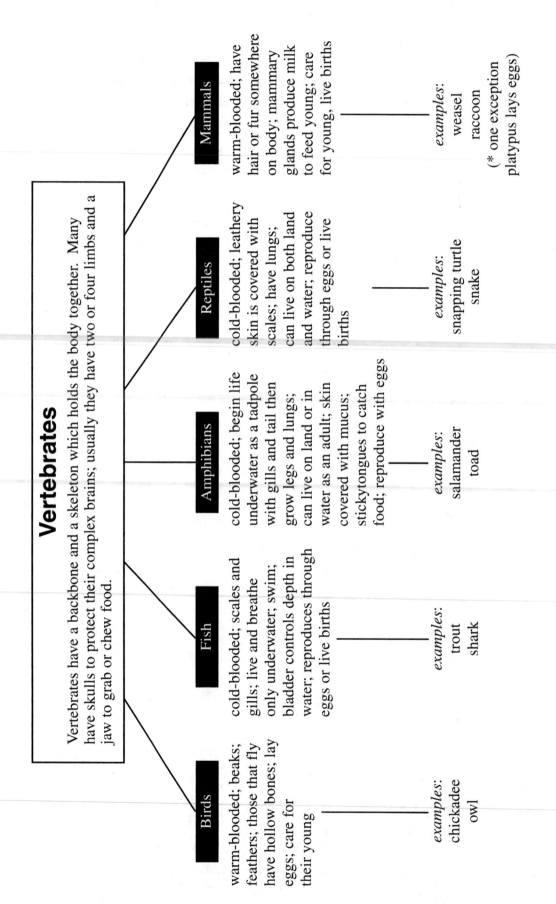

Birds

warm-blooded; beaks; feathers; those that fly have hollow bones; lay eggs; care for their young

examples:
chickadee
owl

Fish

cold-blooded; scales and gills; live and breathe only underwater; swim; bladder controls depth in water; reproduces through eggs or live births

examples:
trout
shark

Amphibians

cold-blooded; begin life underwater as a tadpole with gills and tail then grow legs and lungs; can live on land or in water as an adult; skin covered with mucus; stickytongues to catch food; reproduce with eggs

examples:
salamander
toad

Reptiles

cold-blooded; leathery skin is covered with scales; have lungs; can live on both land and water; reproduce through eggs or live births

examples:
snapping turtle
snake

Mammals

warm-blooded; have hair or fur somewhere on body; mammary glands produce milk to feed young; care for young, live births

examples:
weasel
raccoon
(* one exception platypus lays eggs)

Animal Kingdom

all breathe, reproduce, use senses, eat plants and/or other animals, and usually can move their body

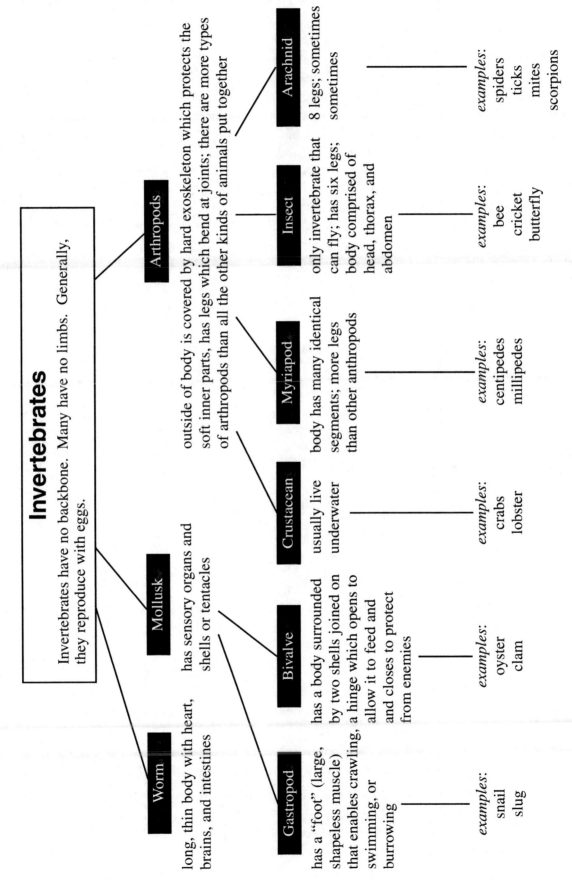

Invertebrates

Invertebrates have no backbone. Many have no limbs. Generally, they reproduce with eggs.

Worm

long, thin body with heart, brains, and intestines

Mollusk

has sensory organs and shells or tentacles

Gastropod

has a "foot" (large, shapeless muscle) that enables crawling, swimming, or burrowing

examples: snail slug

Bivalve

has a body surrounded by two shells joined on a hinge which opens to allow it to feed and and closes to protect from enemies

examples: oyster clam

Arthropods

outside of body is covered by hard exoskeleton which protects the soft inner parts, has legs which bend at joints; there are more types of arthropods than all the other kinds of animals put together

Crustacean

usually live underwater

examples: crabs lobster

Myriapod

body has many identical segments; more legs than other arthropods

examples: centipedes millipedes

Insect

only invertebrate that can fly; has six legs; body comprised of head, thorax, and abdomen

examples: bee cricket butterfly

Arachnid

8 legs; sometimes sometimes

examples: spiders ticks mites scorpions

Reader's Response Journal

As an active process that requires students to put their thoughts, feelings, and ideas into words, writing often helps clarify thinking. To build greater meaning and personal understanding of *My Side of the Mountain*, have each student create a reader's response journal, which will provide them with a written record of their thoughts as they progress through the book. Requiring journals ensures that all students respond to what they've read. A reader's response journal encourages the students to go back and reread passages of the novel and to reflect upon what they've read. Such reflection promotes personal involvement with the book by stimulating students to react to the characters, conflicts, actions, and events. Here are a few ideas for using reader's response journals in your classroom.

- Discuss the purpose of reader's response journals. Motivate the class by encouraging the students to use their journals as a way to express their personal feelings about the book and related issues in their own lives.

- Using passages from the book, model the journal-writing process for the class. Show students how you would record your own feelings, thoughts, ideas, observations, and questions about what you've read.

- Emphasize to the students that you are the only person besides themselves who will see the journal entries; they will not be required to share them with classmates.

- To encourage risk-taking and creative expression, be sure to explain that you will not be grading the grammar, spelling, or writing mechanics in the entries.

- Provide students with journal starters such as these:
  - ❏ It's hard for me to imagine . . .
  - ❏ If (event from the story) happened to me, I would . . .
  - ❏ This reminds me of . . .
  - ❏ I've felt the same way that Sam does when . . .
  - ❏ I don't understand why . . .
  - ❏ While reading this section, I learned . . .
  - ❏ I thought it was wrong for Sam to . . .

- Locate three passages from the section the class is working on. Invite your students to choose which of these passages they feel most interested in responding to and have them write their response. Here are some examples from Section 1:
  - ❏ "The land is no place for a Gribley, and here I am 300 feet from the beech with *Gribley* carved on it."
  - ❏ "I can talk about that first night now, although it is still embarrassing to me because I was so stupid and scared, that I hate to admit it."
  - ❏ ". . . I was stuffed on catfish. I have since learned to cook it more, but never have I enjoyed a meal as much as that one, and never have I felt so independent again."

- Have volunteers share their responses. Never require a student to share an entry with the class. Provide feedback to the students, gently encouraging greater clarity, if necessary. Since response journals are about the students' feelings and opinions, it's crucial that you accept whatever they've written even if you disagree.

Quiz Time

Teacher Note: *Each quiz question indicates which level of Bloom's taxonomy it addresses: K = knowledge, C = comprehension, AP = application, AN = analysis, S = synthesis, and E = evaluation.*

Directions: Read each question and answer on the lines provided.

1. Who is Frightful? (*K*) _____

   _____

2. Describe Sam's dwelling. (*C*) _____

   _____

3. Why does Sam find it so distressing to help the old lady pick strawberries? (*AP*) _____

   _____

4. Why is Sam anxious about the fire warden? (*AN*) _____

   _____

5. What do all of Sam's traps for catching food have in common? (*S*) _____

   _____

   _____

6. Do you think it was wise of Sam to steal the baby falcon from her nest? Why or why not? (*E*)

   _____

7. How does Sam preserve extra fish so he can eat them later? (*K*) _____

   _____

8. How does Sam learn the information he needs to know about falcons? (*C*) _____

   _____

   _____

9. How does Sam use hickory sticks? (*AP*) _____

   _____

10. Describe the similarities between Sam and The Baron. (*AN*) _____

    _____

    _____

11. What might have happened if the mother falcon had continued her attack on Sam? (*S*) _____

    _____

12. Do you think it was right of Sam to hide the dead deer from the poacher? Why or why not? (*E*)

    _____

Design a Mobile

A mobile is perfect for illustrating groups or clusters of ideas. Make your mobile eye-catching by paying attention to color and shape as well as relating your pictures to a theme or title. Choose a title relating to *My Side of the Mountain* and a theme you want to represent in your drawings. Examples of possible themes include the animals and people that Sam befriends and meets on the mountain, the different things that Sam has to learn to make and to do to survive on the mountain, etc.

Materials (for each student)

- a list of concepts or ideas relating to a theme from the book to illustrate
- paper plate
- yarn, string, or ribbon
- cardboard or poster board

- markers or paints
- a dowel about 8" (20 cm) long or an unsharpened pencil
- scissors
- stapler or glue

Directions

1. Using your list and the cardboard or poster board, draw each item for your mobile.

2. Paint or color the items. As you cut them out, be aware of the shape, or silhouette, of each example. This will be the first thing people notice about your mobile, so be creative.

3. Cut a length of string or ribbon about 18" (46 cm) long. Attach one end of it to the center of the pencil or dowel by wrapping it a few times around and securing it with a knot.

4. Make a small hole in the center of the paper plate. Thread the free end of the string through the hole in the center of the paper plate and pull it through, drawing the dowel or pencil tightly against the plate. Tie a knot in the upper end of the string. The pencil and dowel should be on the underside of the plate. This step will provide support for your items and make a strong hanger for your finished work.

5. Using string or ribbon and a stapler or glue, attach the parts of the mobile to the outside rim of the paper plate. You may use various lengths of string or ribbon for these parts, but just make sure that your items are balanced properly so that the finished project does not lean to one side.

6. Use the knotted end of the string to suspend your mobile, allowing it to move freely.

Cause and Effect

Materials

- marker
- tape
- at least one 3" x 5" (8 cm x 13 cm) card with a cause or an effect for every student in the class (If you have an odd number, you will need to participate; if you have fewer than 28 students, you will need to eliminate enough of the causes and effects to have the correct total number for your class.)

Directions

1. Copy one of the following causes or effects from page 20 onto each card. Do not indicate whether it is a cause or an effect, and do not include the numbers. For each cause that you write on a card, be sure to include the corresponding effect on another card.

2. Distribute a card to each student in the class. Half of the students will have causes; the other half will have effects.

3. Have the students tape the statements on their chests.

4. The student with an effect must find the person with the appropriate cause; the student with a cause must find the person with the appropriate effect.

5. Once the students are paired up, call each pair up. Have them stand so that the cause is on the left and the effect is on the right. The one with the cause reads his or her statement aloud and then the one with the effect reads his or hers aloud.

6. Lead a discussion, if necessary, for clarification or to help the class see the relationship.

7. An extension activity would be to have the students determine the true chronological order of the events. (**Note:** First discuss how the book begins with the storm and then has a long flashback section.)

Sam visits Miss Turner and researches falcons.

Sam reluctanctly picks berries as slowly as he possibly can.

Cause and Effect *(cont.)*

Causes	Effects
1. Sam tells his father that he intends to run away to his great-grandfather's land.	1. Sam's dad laughs at him and doesn't take him seriously.
2. Sam's second handmade wooden fishhook works.	2. Sam catches five little trout.
3. Sam cannot get a fire started with the flint and steel.	3. Sam doesn't get to cook the trout he caught.
4. Sam makes a temporary hemlock bough bed for his first night in the stream valley.	4. The cold winds blowing through the valley keep Sam awake all night long.
5. Sam finds Bill, who cooks the fish he caught.	5. Bill helps Sam learn how to successfully start a fire.
6. Sam asks the librarian for help locating the Gribley land.	6. Miss Turner draws a map which leads Sam to his mountain.
7. Sam encounters a little old lady who insists he help her pick strawberries.	7. Sam reluctantly picks berries as slowly as he possibly can.
8. Sam visits Miss Turner and researches falcons.	8. Sam learns how to take care of a baby falcon and train it to catch food for him.
9. The mother falcon dives at Sam as he perches on a cliff.	9. Sam throws out his foot so that his tennis shoe takes the blow.
10. After removing Frightful from her nest, Sam scrambles down the cliff.	10. Frightful digs her talons into Sam's skin.
11. Sam sees a man in a forester's uniform near his tree.	11. Sam builds a lean-to near the gorge and spends the rest of the day and all night there with Frightful.
12. Sam catches a weasel in one of his traps.	12. The Baron flies out at Sam, runs up to his head, and yanks on his hair.
13. Sam puts some hickory sticks and water into a tin can and boils them.	13. Sam ends up with a black salt that he uses to season his food.
14. Sam sees the first winter storm coming.	14. Sam grabs Frightful's straps and dives through his deerskin door into his tree.

Plant and Fungi Classifications

Preparation

1. Prepare an enlarged version of the graphic organizer shown on the next page without the information filled in and place it on a bulletin board or wall where all the students can see it.

2. Teach a lesson about the divisions and classifications of the plant and fungi kingdoms. As you discuss the kingdoms, fill in the graphic organizer with the class.

3. Have the students copy the graphic organizer and information into their own notes.

4. Then have the students do the activity described below.

Materials

- 62 blank 3" x 5" (8 cm x 13 cm) cards
- fishing line or string
- tagboard or poster board
- scissors
- glue

Directions

1. Write a plant or name from the examples given on page 40 or a fungi name from the bottom of page 22 on each of the blank cards before beginning this activity.

2. Divide the students into groups of four.

3. Assign each cooperative group one of the groups (fern, mosses, etc.) from the plant kingdom.

4. The students need to draw their plant group's name on tagboard or poster board using letters that are about 18" (46 cm) high. Cut out the name.

5. Hang the names from the ceiling with the fishing line or string, or place them on the bulletin board or a large wall.

6. Distribute the cards with the plant names to the class members.

7. Ask the students to glue the cards onto the letters in the group name to which the plant belongs. They will probably need to trim the cards to fit the letters.

8. If a student does not know what group his or her plant belongs to, he or she may discuss it with the group members or look it up in an encyclopedia.

Plant Kingdom

all have roots, leaves, and stems and make their own food through photosynthesis

Vascular

have internal conducting tubes that bring water from roots up the stem to the rest of the plant

Anthophyta (Flowering plants)

most reproduce through seeds encased in pods or fruit

examples: deciduous trees, bushes, and flower

includes plants that reproduce through bulbs, tubers, runners, and rhizomes

examples: iris, strawberries, and daffodils

Gymnosperm (Coniferous)

needle-like leaves; produce resin; seeds encased in cones; produce both male and female cones; male cones release pollen which fertilize female cones' seeds

examples: hemlock, fir cypress, and cedar

Ferns

two types of leaves:

- fertile, produce pores
- sterile, only do photosynthesis

Non-vascular

Moss and Liverworts

must live in moist areas; reproduce through spores and gametes; have tiny stems and leaves

Fungi Kingdom

absorb nutrients from their environment; root-like tissues called hyphae

reproduce through spores

has no leaves, stems, roots, or chlorophyll; cannot do photosynthesis

examples: mushrooms, puffballs, and mold

* *Teacher Note: Up until the late 1990s, fungi were classified with plants. They are now their own kingdom because they really don't fit the criteria for plants.*

Learn to Do Library Research

Sam Gribley relies on the Delhi Public Library for crucial information that allows him to be successful in the wilderness: first to locate his great grandfather's property and later to learn all he can about falcons and their training.

Library skills have taken on greater improtance today than ever before. The World Wide Web has shown us that no one can ever hope to know all there is to know and the ability to locate desired information is the essential skill of the 21st century. Therefore, ask each student to choose one of the following topics to research.

- peregrine falcon   • Catskill Mountains   • wilderness survival

Next, write the following list of reference materials on the board.

❑ encyclopedia (bound, CD, or online)   ❑ microfilm/microfiche

❑ dictionary   ❑ *Readers's Guide to Periodical Literature* (bound or online)

❑ thesaurus

❑ atlas   ❑ catalog of library holdings (online or card catalog)

❑ almanac

❑ *Guiness Book of Records*

Present the questions below to the class, asking students to identify the reference source(s) that would most likely provide the answer.

- What could you use to find out how far it is from New York City to Delhi, New York?

- What could you use to find out if any articles have been written about training falcons in the last five years?

- What could you use to read a newspaper article from four years ago?

- What could you use to locate a detailed map of the Catskill Mountains?

- What could you use to find out the longest time period of anyone has ever survived in the wilderness?

- During you research you encounter the word *peregrine* and need to know its meaning. What reference would you use?

- What source could you use to find out what books in the library have information on the Catskills?

- You want a synonym for the word *prey* so you won't have to say the same word repeatedly during your talk. What reference source would you use?

When you have covered all the materials and their usage, allow the students time in the library to research thier topics.

Students should prepare a three-minute talk about what they learned about their topic. They can present their speeches to the class or record them on a tape recorder for you to review at a convenient time. Students must submit a list of the reference materials they used. This can just be a list of titles and doesn't need to be written in bibliographical format.

Quiz Time

Teacher Note: *Each quiz question indicates which level of Bloom's taxonomy it addresses: K = knowledge, C = comprehension, AP = application, AN = analysis, S = synthesis, and E = evaluation.*

Directions: Read each question and answer on the lines provided.

1. What is Sam training Frightful to do? (K) _____

_____

2. How does Sam prepare the deer hide so he can make the things he needs from it? (C) _____

_____

3. Name three ways that summer makes Sam's life on the mountain easier than the spring. (AP) ____

_____

4. Why do you think Sam awakened "Bando"? (AN) _____

_____

5. Besides the deerskin, what else could Sam have used for a door to his home? (S) _____

_____

6. Of the foods that Sam eats in the wilderness, which would you be willing to try? Explain why. (E)

_____

7. Name three new things Sam made for the first time. (K) _____

_____

8. Describe three steps in Frightful's training. (C) _____

_____

_____

9. What did you learn about fireplaces from Sam's scary experience with Frightful? (AP) _____

_____

10. Describe the similarities between "Bando" and "Thoreau." (AN) _____

_____

11. What do Jesse Coon James, The Baron, and Frightful all have in common? (S) _____

_____

12. Do you think Sam's decision to not return to school in September was wise? Explain why or why not. (E) _____

_____

Sam's Mountain

Directions: Sam gives a vivid description of his mountain and a rough sketch is given at the beginning of the book. Using this information and your imagination, recreate Sam's mountain in one of the following ways:

- ❑ Using watercolors, pastels, or markers, create a detailed landscape picture.
- ❑ Build the mountain using paper-mâché over a wire frame, modeling clay, or sculpting dough (recipe provided below).

You must include the following important details in your drawing or model, you can add any other details you'd like:

- Sam's tree
- the grove of huge old trees and boulders
- Sam's "bathtub" spring
- the gorge
- the stream
- the meadow

Helpful Hints for Building Models

- ✦ A wooden board will support the model's weight better than a cardboard one.
- ✦ Use real twigs/branches for trees (especially pine trees, where you can cut the needles quite short).
- ✦ To provide a realistic ground covering, glue soil, moss, blades of grass, or crushed real leaves to the model.
- ✦ Glue real pebbles on the model (for large rocks and boulders); this is especially effective for defining the gorge.
- ✦ Use modeling clay to create Sam, the Baron, Jesse Coon James, and a deer. Place them on the model.
- ✦ Think of special touches you can add—for example, a campfire made of tiny sticks glued in a triangular fashion and surrounded by a circle of tiny pebbles; stacks of firewood stacked up outside Sam's tree.
- ✦ When using the sculpting dough, you can get a stronger model if you build it around an underlying structure such as a toilet/paper towel tube covered with foil or plastic wrap.

Sculpting Dough Recipe

(This will make enough dough for one mountain model.)

Ingredients

- 4 cups (960 mL) flour
- 1 1/2 cups (360 mL) warm water
- 2 cups (480 mL) table salt*
- food coloring (if desired)
- 2 T (30 mL) cooking oil

Directions

Combine wet ingredients and food coloring, if desired (red and green make brown). Add dry ingredients and mix well. Knead well with floured hands. Then store in an airtight bag or covered container until ready to use. After creating the sculpture, you can speed up its hardening by placing the model on a cookie sheet in a preheated 200°F (90°C) oven for 5 to 10 minutes.

(Note: Do not use reduced sodium salt.)

Become a Team of Experts

Directions

1. Gather books about plants and animals. Have encyclopedias available.

2. Place the students in groups of three. Since these groups must work closely together and later serve as a panel of experts fielding questions from class members, consider the group's makeup carefully.

3. Assign each group one of these categories from the plant or animal kingdom:

mosses and liverworts	anthropod	reptile
anthophyta	worm	mollusk
ferns	fish	amphibian
gymnosperm	bird	mammal

4. If you don't have enough groups, you'll need to decide which of these categories to omit and adjust the group size accordingly. (For example, if you want to concentrate on just the plant kingdom, you may want to include fungi and increase the group size to five.)

5. Define the word "experts" for the groups (people who are highly knowledgeable about a specific subject). Then tell the groups that they are to become experts on the category they have been given. If you plan to do the Stump the Experts activity (page 31), explain that they will have to answer difficult questions about their topic.

6. The groups' first source of information (to get started) should be the graphic organizers (animal or plant kingdoms) you completed as a class.

7. Students should discuss their findings with one another and prepare an outline, note cards, or graphic organizer summarizing the information gathered by the group.

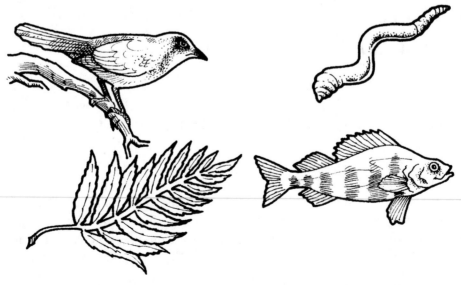

Writing in the Active Voice

Sentences written in the active voice are more interesting and powerful for a reader than sentences written in the passive voice. Eliminating "to be" verbs changes a sentence from the passive to the active voice. With this fact in mind, skilled authors like Jean Craighead George choose their words carefully. Even so, a few sentences in *My Side of the Mountain* have some "to be" verbs that could have been eliminated.

Here's an example.

Passive Voice—"It was good to be whistling and carefree again, because I was sure scared by the coming of that storm."

Active Voice—It felt good to whistle and feel carefree again, because the coming of that storm had terrified me.

Directions: Rewrite these sentences in the active voice by getting rid of as many "to be" verbs as possible. You want to eliminate these words: *was, were, are, am, is, be, being, been.*

1. "I did not get a fire going that night, and as I mentioned, this was a scary experience."

   _____

2. ". . . I was depending on fish to keep me alive until I got to my great-grandfather's mountain, where I was going to make traps and catch game."

   _____

   _____

3. "I was immediately cheered, and set out directly for the highway."

   _____

4. "Sam Gribley, if you are going to run off and live in the woods, you better learn how to make a fire."

   _____

5. ". . . he thought I'd be home the next day." _____

6. "I finally got a handful of dried grass to burn. Grass is even better than pine needles, and tomorrow I am going to try the outside bark of the river birch."

   _____

   _____

7. "I found a marsh. In it there were cattails and arrow-leaf . . ."

   _____

8. "Somewhere around here was great-grandfather's beech tree with the name Gribley carved on it."

   _____

9. "I ate a flower. It was not very good." _____

10. "If the animal life can eat it, it is safe for humans." _____

   _____

My Family Tree

Sam had heard so much about Great-Grandfather Gribley's farm that he longed to go there and experience it for himself. What do you know about your ancestors or their lives? Find out all you can about your family and fill in the names of your ancestors on a family tree that you design. Use the family tree below as a model or guide. On a separate sheet of paper, write two paragraphs about an ancestor who particularly interests you.

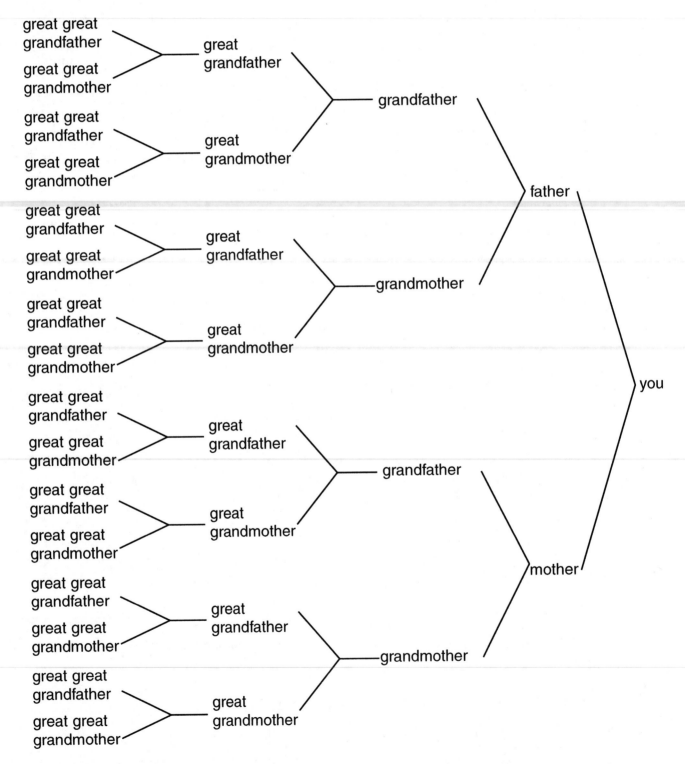

Quiz Time

Teacher Note: *Each quiz question indicates which level of Bloom's taxonomy it addresses: K = knowledge, C = comprehension, AP = application, AN = analysis, S = synthesis, and E = evaluation.*

Directions: Read each question carefully and write the answer on the lines provided.

1. What does Sam do when he realizes it's Halloween? (*K*) _____

    _____

2. Describe Sam's cold-weather clothing. (*C*)_____

    _____

3. If Sam hadn't acquired a deer hide, what else might he have used for a blanket? (*AP*) _____

    _____

4. Does Sam's Halloween party turn out the way he anticipated? Explain. (*AN*) _____

    _____

5. What caused Sam to go into town and start a conversation with "Mr. Jacket"? (*S*) _____

    _____

6. Do you think it was a good idea for Sam to head to the library during the hunting season?
    Explain. (*E*) _____

    _____

7. What does Sam suddenly realize he needs lots of in order to make it safely through the winter
    months? (*K*) _____

    _____

8. How does Sam justify hiding the deer from the hunters who shot them? (*C*) _____

    _____

9. Predict what may happen now that Sam has been seen in town. (*AP*) _____

    _____

10. What made tanning the deer hides Sam got in November more difficult than the one he had gotten
    in the summer? (*AN*) _____

    _____

11. What might Sam have done if "Mr. Jacket" had followed him from town? (*S*) _____

    _____

12. Do you think Sam is going to make it through the winter living in his tree? Explain. (*E*)

    _____

Create a Model of Sam's Tree Home

Sam spends a lot of time inside his tree home, so Jean Craighead George gives us an extensive description of the tree and its contents.

Directions: Reread the section of the book that tells about Sam's home, his bed, and his fireplace. Glance through the entire book and study any drawings of his tree house that you come across. Try to envision Sam's tree home in your mind Sketch out a plan of your model using the space below. Make a model of Sam's tree home.

Here are a few material suggestions to get you started:

- empty cardboard canisters (especially oatmeal ones) or paper-mâché and chicken wire
- brown fabric, tissue paper, or construction paper
- actual bark (Use dead wood—please don't strip a live tree or branch.)
- small twigs and craft sticks (for creating the bed)
- modeling clay and flat pebbles (for fireplace)
- tan felt or fabric (for door and Sam's "blanket")

Use your imagination and enjoy!

Stump the Experts

Teacher Note: This is a follow-up activity to Become a Team of Experts on page 26.

Preparation

In this activity, you will reconvene the teams of experts formed in the activity on page 26. Arrange a line of desks or a long table at the front of the room with the rest of the desks and chairs facing it (similar to a panel discussion).

Directions

1. Call up a team of experts to sit at the panel table. They should bring any materials they have prepared based on their research.

2. The class will try to stump the panel. They should ask questions that they think the panel may not be able to answer. Reproduce the question form below and distribute copies to students not on the panel. They can use the form to write their questions ahead of time.

3. When everyone is ready, class members take turns standing to ask a question. The panel members may confer on answers. (This allows everyone to have a chance to participate.)

4. When every class member has had a chance to "stump the panel," the next team of experts comes up and the questioning continues. Continue until all teams have been questioned.

5. The score is kept by giving one point to the panel of experts for each correctly answered question. The panel is not penalized for the inability to answer a question. The panel of experts with the most points wins.

- -

Question Form

Questions for _____

(Panel Member's Name)

Question: _____

_____

_____

Question: _____

_____

_____

Question: _____

_____

_____

Math Word Problems

Directions: Sam had to use his wits to survive on the mountain for an entire year. Use your wits to find the answers to the following questions. Be sure to show your work and include a label with your answers.

1. It is the last day of September. Sam eats about 23 walnuts daily. How many should he gather to see him through from October to the end of April?

2. It takes Sam two weeks to prepare the deer hide so that it is soft enough to make into a piece of clothing and another 16 days to sew it. When should he begin this process if he wants to have a pair of gloves by October 31?

3. It takes Sam six hours to collect and cut a cord of wood for his clay fireplace. He estimates that he will need about 115 cords to see him through the cold months of autumn, winter, and early spring. How many hours will he need to work to get enough wood?

4. There are an average of 15 trees on every acre of Gribley land. There are 32 acres on the mountain. About how many trees are on the mountain?

5. Sam believes five percent of the trees on the mountain were ruined by the ice storm. About how many trees survived the ice storm?

6. The time from when Sam ran away until his parents came to him on the mountain totaled 372 days. How many hours was he on his own (rounded to the nearest tens)?

Create Portmanteau Words

Skillful authors sometimes invent new words when they feel there is no appropriate word in our language for what they want to say. These words are called *portmanteau words*.

Portmanteau means combining two words to create a new word. Two portmanteau words you might know are:

> **chortle** (a combination of chuckle and snort)
>
> **scurrying** (a combination of hurrying and scramble)

Jean Craighead George included several portmanteau words in *My Side of the Mountain*.

Directions: Read the quotes below. Highlight (or underline) the portmanteau word in each. On the lines provided, write the two words you believe the author combined.

_____ + _____ 1. "He came down headfirst to our private bath, a scrabbly, skinny young raccoon."

_____ + _____ 2. "Small pinfeathers were sticking out of (Frightful's) stroobly down, like feathers in an Indian quiver."

_____ + _____ 3. ". . . a scuttering and scraping of boots on the rocks."

_____ + _____ 4. "Frightful fluffed her nubby feathers and shook."

_____ + _____ 5. "(The raccoon) was chittering . . ."

Now that you understand the concept, try creating two portmanteau words yourself. Use your portmanteau words in a sentence so the reader has a context to understand the word. Challenge your classmates or teacher to figure out the two words you combined by reading the sentence that you created.

1. _____ + _____

_____

_____

2. _____ + _____

_____

_____

Quiz Time

Teacher Note: *Each quiz question indicates which level of Bloom's taxonomy it addresses: K = knowledge,*
C = comprehension, AP = application, AN = analysis, S = synthesis, and E = evaluation.

Directions: Read each question carefully and write the answer on the lines provided.

1. Who comes to visit Sam for Christmas? (*K*) _____

   _____

2. Does Sam think Bando likes the gift he made for him? Explain. (*C*) _____

   _____

3. What are some of the things that Sam does to stay busy during the winter months? List at least three things. (*AP*) _____

   _____

4. How did Sam's father's attitude toward Frightful change during his visit? (*AN*)_____

   _____

5. Why do you think Sam told Matt anything about the "wild boy"? (*S*) _____

   _____

6. Explain a nutritional weakness in Sam's winter diet. (*E*) _____

   _____

7. Who is Tom Sidler, and how does Sam meet him? (*K*) _____

   _____

8. What does Sam do to help the herd of starving deer? Explain. (*C*) _____

   _____

9. What do you think prompted Frightful to fly toward another falcon in the sky? Explain. (*AP*)

   _____

10. Toward the end of the story do you think Sam wanted to be found? Explain. (*AN*) _____

   _____

11. If Sam were to return to New York City, do you think Frightful could be set free in the Catskill Mountains? Explain. (*S*) _____

   _____

12. Did this story seem believable to you? Give at least two reasons why it did or did not. (*E*)

   _____

   _____

Jackdaws

A jackdaw is an unusual bird who collects just about anything it can carry and hordes it in its nest. A jackdaw is just an aviary version of the packrat! As an educational activity, a jackdaw is a collection of things related to a specific topic. Jackdaws have received attention as an instructional tool because they promote higher-level thinking skills in students in an enjoyable way.

Materials

Each student needs a large shoebox (or another large cardboard box).

Directions

1. Each student will create a Jackdaw containing at least five items to remind Sam of his time on the mountain. Each item must include a card stating why the student chose that item.

2. Each student must get up in front of the class and present one item from his or her Jackdaw. The student may read the card he or she prepared. He or she should strive to show an item that no one else has already presented.

3. Jackdaws look terrific in showcases or on display for parents' night or open house. They create a lot of interest throughout the school and for visitors from the community.

Sample

Creative Review Questions

Here is an interesting and fun way for your students to review the novel quickly.

Materials

Each student needs two pieces of blank paper, one marker, and tape.

Directions

1. Assign one chapter (from chapters 1–11) to half of the students in your class (up to 11 students). If there are more than 11 students in half of your class, divide up the chapters.

2. Give the students about six minutes to briefly review (skim) their sections.

3. Each student writes a question based on the material in their assigned chapter on one of the two sheets of paper.

4. The student then writes the answer to that same question on the other sheet of paper.

5. Collect the questions in one stack and the answers in another.

6. Shuffle each stack and give each student in the class one question or one answer. (This is why only half the class is assigned the chapters.)

7. Have the students tape the questions or answers on their chests.

8. The students with questions stand on the left side of the room; the students with answers stand on the right side of the room.

9. The students read the questions or answers on each other's chests and locate the person with whom they belong.

10. The answer person goes to stand with the question person.

11. Call each pair up to the front of the room. Have them stand so that the question and answer are both showing. Have each student read what is written on his or her paper. The student with the question should read first.

12. Lead a discussion, if necessary, for clarification or to help the class review the information.

13. On the same day or at another time, assign chapters 12–22 to the other half of the class to generate the questions and answers so that each student has a chance to create questions and answers.

Figurative Language

Talented writers such as Jean Craighead George use figurative language to make scenes more vivid. In *My Side of the Mountain* she uses these figurative language devices:

- **hyperbole**—an obvious exaggeration: The garbage can was the size of the *Titanic*.

- **simile**—a comparison using the words *like* or *as*: pretty *like* a butterfly; as hungry *as* a bear

- **personification**—giving human characteristics to a nonhuman (plant, animal, or thing):
  The vine *clutched* at her leg and refused to let go.

- **verbification**—using a noun (person, place, or thing) as a verb (action word): The highway
  snaked around the curves of the mountain.

Directions: Read each quote from the book. Decide whether it is an example of hyperbole (*h*),
simile (*s*), personification (*p*), or verbification (*v*), and write the abbreviation for your choice on the line
provided. Then highlight (or underline) the words that indicate to you the type of figurative language
being used.

_____ 1. " . . . I must have walked a thousand miles before I found a pool . . . "

_____ 2. " . . . the whole tree moans right down to the roots . . . "

_____ 3. " . . . the movement of a human being is like the difference between the explosion
of a cap pistol and a cannon."

_____ 4. " . . . and so can I cook my fish here, because I haven't eaten in years."

_____ 5. "It was a clear, athletic stream that rushed and ran and jumped and splashed."

_____ 6. "Inside I felt as cozy as a turtle in its shell."

_____ 7. "Two sentinel boulders guarded . . . a bathtub-sized spring."

_____ 8. "There caterpillaring around boulders, rollercoastering up ravines and down hills
was a mound of rocks that had once been great-grandfather's boundary fence."

_____ 9. "(The trees) must have begun when the world began."

_____ 10. "(The boulders) looked like pebbles beneath those trees."

_____ 11. "I wormed toward camp."

_____ 12. "I was so scared I could see my heart lift my sweater."

_____ 13. "The weasel . . . stood on his hind feet to lecture me again."

Compare Yourself to Sam

The point of reading literature is to gain insight into life as a process for change. What makes a story compelling is exploring that process through its characters. The more an author can have us empathize and relate to the character, the more we feel connected and interested in the book. In addition, through the exploration of a character's change and growth, we can often learn more about ourselves.

Directions: Think about the prompts below and how you would answer them for Sam. Next, think about the prompts below and how you would answer them for yourself. Then complete the Venn diagram. In the left circle, write things that apply only to Sam. In the right circle, write things that apply only to you. In the middle section write things that apply to both of you. You do not need to use all the prompts given, and you can add any other things you'd like.

family size	feelings about books/libraries	fears (and those overcome)
abilities	knowledge	pets
confidence	friends	adventures
need for solitude	desire to escape	independence
favorite foods	willingness to try new things	typical pastimes

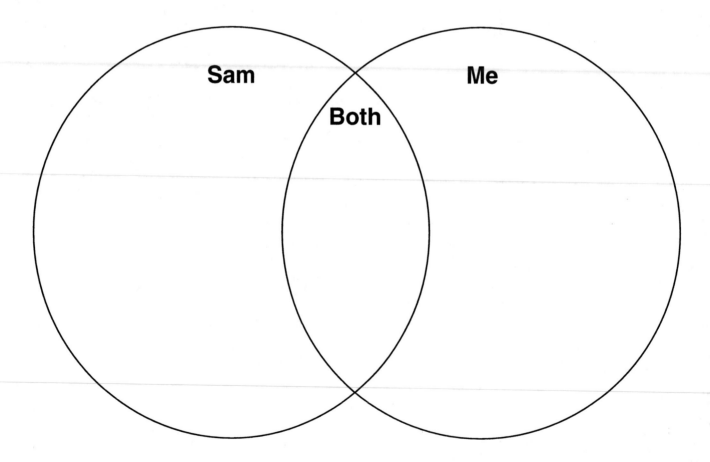

Book Report Ideas

There are many ways to report about a book once you have read it. After you have completed *My Side of the Mountain*, have each student choose one method of reporting on the book, using the ideas given here or any other creative ideas you or the students devise.

Book Character

Choose a character from the book (Bando, Matt Spell, or Sam's dad) and dress up like the character. Tell the class the story from your character's perspective.

Police Report

Write only the facts in a one-page format from the perspective of a police officer. The report will tell the who, what, when, where, why, and how of the story without embellishments, extra details, or any opinions.

Game

A pair of students create a board game based on the events in the story. Be sure to include instructions for play, use of the game board, and all the necessary game pieces.

Into the Future

Write an actual chapter or a summary of what happens next now that Sam's family has come to live on the mountain with him. The student may choose to present this as a dramatization.

News Interview

A pair of students perform this book report as an interview. One student pretends to be Sam, completely immersed in the character. The other student plays the role of a television or newspaper reporter, trying to provide the audience with insights into the character's personality and life. It can be challenging and fun for the partners to create a realistic, meaningful dialogue.

Internet

Write a brief, specific opinion statement about *My Side of the Mountain*. (e.g., "I would recommend this book to a friend because I enjoyed reading about Sam's wilderness adventures," or "I disliked this book because nothing really exciting happened, and I prefer action-packed adventure stories.") Remember that what you write may be read by people worldwide, so "It was neat" is not good enough. Now go to this Web address: *http://www.amazon.com*. Navigate to the book *My Side of the Mountain*, click on "Write a review" (located in the left sidebar), and type in the statement you've prepared. While you're there, check out what other reviewers have said about the book. Do most agree or disagree with what you've written? Share your findings with the class.

Annotation

Although this sounds simple, it is actually quite a challenging task for children: sum up the plot in one sentence without giving the ending away. All American books have a Library of Congress annotation written for them by a trained professional. (e.g., A teenager named Sam runs away from his crowded New York City apartment and survives in the wilderness of the Catskill Mountains.

Video Review

Watch the video of *My Side of the Mountain* (VHS, 1969; rated G). Then compare and contrast the video with the book, describing which parts of each version you preferred.

Culminating Activities

Allow students to choose one of the following culminating activities to demonstrate the knowledge they acquired as a result of reading *My Side of the Mountain*:

Small Group Activities

1. Form a small group of no more than three people. Whittle willow whistles just as Bando and Sam did. Learn to play the songs they played in the book or create a new song. Play the song(s) for the class.

2. Form a small group of no more than three people. Use clay to recreate Sam's clay fireplace and flue.

Individual Activities

1. Write a letter from Sam to Great-Grandpa Gribley telling about Sam's experiences living on the mountain. Write a letter from Great-Grandpa Gribley to Sam telling about experiences you believe he would have had while living on the mountain.

2. Learn how to make blueberry jam and share it with the rest of the class.

3. Pick a funny scene from the book and turn it into a four or five panel comic strip (e.g., when the Baron chased the hikers away; when Sam laughs at Frightful slipping on the ice and then takes a spill himself, etc.)

4. Choose one of the topics below and prepare a 500-word report about it or create a poster or chart to share the information you learn.

Plants					
buttercups	arrow leaf	trillium	mushrooms (fungi)	hawthorn	marsh
jack-in-the-pulpit	dogtooth violets	bloodroot	pennyroyals	teaberry	milkweed
	lima beans	wild onion	winterberry	wintergreen	watercress
strawberries	dandelions	water lily	blueberry	lichens	orris
ferns	skunk cabbage	wild carrot	Solomon's seal	snakewood	
moss	wildflowers	elderberry	sedges	lousewort	
grass	potato	daisy	bulrushes	sorrel	
cattails	garlic	puffballs (fungi)	crowfeet	dock	

Trees				
basswood	beech	dogwood	apple	willow
hemlock	river birch	hickory	poplar	
ash	maple	white birch	slippery elm	
aspen	pine	oak	walnut	

Animals					
fish	turtle	catfish	*peregrine falcon	sparrow	robin
rabbit	trout	warbler	minnow	opposum	cardinal
spider	woodpecker	mussel	snapping turtle	red fox	shrew
crow	junco	crayfish	wood peevee	flying squirrel	salamander
hawk	chickadee	beetle	groundhog	mouse	brown thrasher
squirrel	nuthatch	frog	cricket	skunk	cooper's hawk
weasel	grub	nighthawk	catbird	bat	
racoon	earthworm	chicken	woodthrush	oriole	
deer	whippoorwill	dog	pheasant	vireo	

*A student should not select this if he or she chose peregrine falcon for the library research project on page 23.

Unit Test I

Part I: Matching

Directions: Match the word to its synonym. Not all choices are used.

_____ 1. emphatic	A. annoyed	H. scolded
_____ 2. ravine	B. thicket	I. secretly
_____ 3. berated	C. consume	J. tasty
_____ 4. savory	D. insistent	K. boring
_____ 5. tedious	E. confident	L. frightening
_____ 6. copse	F. unusual	M. ridiculous
_____ 7. furtively	G. forceful	N. valley
_____ 8. sanguine		
_____ 9. devour		
_____ 10. resounding		

Part II: True/False

Directions: Read each statement. Write True or False on the line.

_____ 1. Sam's first night on his own goes well.

_____ 2. Sam learns how to start a fire all by himself.

_____ 3. Miss Turner helps Sam to locate his Great Grandpa Gribley's property.

_____ 4. Sam finds a baby falcon who fell out of her nest and nurses her back to health.

_____ 5. The Baron is not afraid of Sam.

_____ 6. Sam avoids capture by the fire warden.

_____ 7. Sam hides dead deer so that the hunters who shot them cannot find them.

_____ 8. Sam has great difficulty finding anything edible on the mountain.

_____ 9. Sam has a problem making his fireplace functional.

_____ 10. Sam discovers how to make blueberry jam on his own.

_____ 11. Sam spends the week after Christmas alone.

_____ 12. The ice storm destroys Sam's home.

_____ 13. Numerous newspaper articles are printed regarding Sam.

_____ 14. Sam refuses to talk to Matt Spell about the "wild boy."

_____ 15. At the end of the story, Sam's entire family moves to the mountain.

Unit Test II

Directions: Here are some quotations from *My Side of the Mountain*. Choose 10 of the following quotes and thoroughly explain the meaning of each on a separate sheet of paper.

Chapter 1

"I cooked them (acorn pancakes) on the top of a tin can, and as I ate them, smothered with blueberry jam, I knew that the land was just the place for a Gribley."

Chapter 9

"(The weasel) flew right out at me, landed on my shoulder, gave me a lecture I shall never forget, and vanished . . . "

Chapter 10

"I don't know why, but this seemed like one of the nicest things I had learned in the woods—that earthworms, lowly, confined to the darkness of the earth—could make just a little stir in the world."

Chapter 12

"Bando said, 'Thoreau, I have led a varied life . . . to me it has been an interesting life. Just now it seems very dull.'"

Chapter 13

"September blazed a trail into the mountains."

Chapter 14

"Never had there been a more real Halloween night."

Chapter 19

"It's surprising how you watch (weather) when you live in it. Not a cloud passed unnoticed, not a wind blew untested."

Chapter 19

"Hunger is a funny thing. It has an intelligence all its own."

Chapter 20

"I told (Matt Spell) that I didn't recommend anyone try to live off the land unless they liked oysters and spinach."

Chapter 20

"Frightful spoke in my head, however, and said, 'You really want to be found or you would not have told Matt all you did.' "

Chapter 21

"There are people in the city who are lonelier than I."

Chapter 22

"(My mother) looked at the mountain and the meadow and the gorge, and I felt her feet squeeze into the earth and take root."

Unit Test III

Choose five of the following situations. Work with a partner to write the conversations that might have occurred in each situation. Each conversation should be at least six sentences long.

- Sam tells his father about his plans to live on the old Gribley farm.

- Sam talks to Bill about his early experiences living in the wilderness.

- Sam explains to a fire warden how he happens to be on the mountain.

- Bando explains to his parents why he won't be spending Christmas with them.

- The authorities from Sam's school phone his parents to ask why he hasn't come back to school.

- Sam describes training Frightful to his father.

- Sam's father tells Sam's mother about his visit with Sam.

- Sam explains to Frightful why he can't let her go free.

- A person in Delhi who saw Sam in town wearing his deerskin suit calls a newspaper reporter to tell what she or he has seen.

- Matt Spell explains to his mom and dad how he's going to spend his spring vacation.

- Miss Turner is questioned by reporters.

- Sam's mother and father discuss moving the family to the mountain.

- Sam talks with his parents about what needs to be done for the family to survive on the mountain.

Bibliography and Related Resources

Other books in the *My Side of the Mountain* Trilogy

George, Jean Craighead. *On the Far Side of the Mountain.* Puffin, 1991 (paperback); E. P. Dutton, 1990 (hardcover). This sequel to *My Side of the Mountain* details what Sam does after Frightful is confiscated and his younger sister Alice disappears from his mountain.

George, Jean Craighead. *Frightful's Mountain.* Dutton Books, 1999. The final book in the trilogy describes Frightful's trials and triumphs after Sam is forced to release her into the wild.

Related books by Jean Craighead George

George, Jean Craighead. *Julie.* Harper Trophy, 1996 (paperback); HarperCollins Juvenile Books, 1997 (hardcover). In this sequel to *Julie of the Wolves*, Julie's new life in her father's village is thrown into turmoil when her beloved wolf pack threatens the herd of musk ox necessary for the people's survival.

George, Jean Craighead. *Julie of the Wolves.* Harper Trophy, 1974 (paperback); HarperCollins Juvenile Books, 1987 (hardcover). A teenage Eskimo girl runs away from an intolerable home situation, becomes lost in the wilds of Alaska, and eventually gets adopted into a pack of Arctic wolves.

George, Jean Craighead. *Julie's Wolf Pack.* HarperCollins Juvenile Books, 1997 (hardcover); HarperCollins Juvenile Books, 1999 (paperback). This final book in the trilogy about Julie and her wolves gives the story of the wolf pack told completely from the wolves' point of view.

George, Jean Craighead. *The Epic Adventures of Julie and Her Wolves.* Harper Trophy, 1999. A compilation of all three Julie novels.

Wilderness Survival Fiction

Hobbs, Will. *Far North.* Avon Camelot, 1997 (paperback); William Morrow and Co., 1996 (hardcover). After a plane crash, two teenage boys struggle to survive during winter in the wilds of Canada's Northwest Territory.

Mazer, Harry. *Snow Bound.* Dell Publishing, 1975 (paperback); Peter Smith Publishers, 1986 (hardcover). A teenage boy and girl caught in a blizzard on a road isolated from civilization must fight the elements to survive.

O'Dell, Scott. *Island of the Blue Dolphins.* Yearling Books, 1987 (paperback); Houghton Mufflin Juvenile, 1990 (hardcover); unrated VHS video, 1964. A fictional work based on the true story of a Native American teenage girl who lives a solitary life for almost 20 years on an island off the California coast.

Paulsen, Gary. *Brian's Winter.* Laureleaf, 1998 (paperback); Delacorte Publishers, 1996 (hardcover). This sequel to *Hatchet* explains what would have happened if Brian had had to spend the winter in the wilderness.

Bibliography and Related Resources *(cont.)*

Wilderness Survival Fiction *(cont.)*

Paulsen, Gary. *Hatchet.* Aladdin Paperbacks, 1996; Simon & Schuster Juvenile, 1987 (hardcover). Thirteen-year-old Brian struggles to survive for two months in northern Canada after a plane crash leaves him alone with only the clothes he has on and a hatchet.

Speare, Elizabeth. *The Sign of the Beaver.* Yearling Books, 1994 (paperback); Houghton Mifflin, 19 (hardcover). A young teen gets separated from his pioneer family in a dense New England forest but survives with the assistance of the Native Americans who befriend him.

Taylor, Theodore. *The Cay.* Camelot, 1995 (paperback); Doubleday, 1987 (hardcover). As the result of a terrifying shipwreck, a young teenager loses his sight and becomes marooned on a Caribbean island where he survives with the help of a wise old Black West Indian sailor.

Wilderness Survival Nonfiction

Churchill, James E. *Basic Essentials Survival.* Glove Pequot Press, 1999. This handbook explains how to survive in the wilderness by telling how to forage and trap food, build a shelter, start a fire without matches, find sources of potable drinking water, and signal for help.

McManners, Hugh. *Outdoor Adventure Handbook.* DK Publishers, 1996. This book explains all the minute details of successfully camping in the wilderness.

Olsen, Larry Dean. *Outdoor Survival Skills.* Chicago Review Press, 1997. This book teaches how to survive in many outdoor environments with little or no equipment.

Storm, Rory. *The Extreme Survival Guide.* Element, 1999. This book appeals to children and teaches important safety advice. Essential adventure survival skills are taught and real life stories of survival are described.

Related Web Sites

Jean Craighead George Web Site
http://www.jeancraigheadgeorge.com

The Aviary
http://www.theaviary.com

National Geographic
http://www.nationalgeographic.com

ThinkQuest *Virtual Zoo*
http://library.thinkquest.org/11922/index.htm

Answer Key

Page 10

1. The setting is Gribley's farm on a mountain in the Catskills sometime between 1930 and 1950.

2. Sam runs away because he hates the overcrowded city apartment and longs for independence.

3. Sam's personality traits include the following: resourceful, independent, confident, knowledgeable, adventurous, etc.

4. Sam was terrified by the coming of the snowstorm but elated that he made it through once it was over.

5. Many things go wrong on Sam's first night, including the following: he doesn't get a fire started, his first fish hook breaks, he can't cook his fish, he is hungry, he is cold, and a whippoorwill keeps him awake all night, etc.

6. Accept reasonable and supported answers.

7. The Baron is a weasel Sam meets when he catches him in a trap.

8. Sam goes to the Delhi library, and a librarian helps him locate it in an old book and even draws him a map.

9. Accept reasonable and supported answers.

10. Bill and Miss Turner were the most helpful to Sam. Bill taught him how to make fire, and Miss Turner drew him the map that led him to his mountain.

11. Accept reasonable and supported answers.

12. Accept reasonable and supported answers.

Page 17

1. Frightful is Sam's trained falcon.

2. Sam lives inside a burned-out, huge, old hemlock tree.

3. Sam feels that the strawberries belong to him, and he was counting on eating them.

4. Sam fears that the fire warden has come to bring him back to civilization.

5. Sam uses bait (food) in all of his traps to lure the animals to the spot.

6. Accept reasonable and supported answers.

7. Sam smokes the extra fish over a fire in order to preserve them.

8. Sam goes to the Delhi library and reads all about falcons.

9. Sam boils hickory sticks to get salt to season his food.

10. Sam and The Baron are alike because they are both playful, adventurous, and independent. They are not afraid of each other, and they enjoy being together, etc.

11. Accept reasonable and supported answers.

12. Accept reasonable and supported answers.

Page 24

1. Sam is training Frightful to catch food for him.

2. Sam soaks the deer hide in tannic acid by placing it in water inside an oak stump. Then he has to chew, twist, and jump on it to soften it up enough to work with.

3. Life is easier for Sam in the summer because plants are more plentiful, fruit is available, Frightful can capture food, and he has Bando for company, etc.

4. Sam awoke Bando so he could talk to another person and tell him all about the mountain.

5. Accept reasonable and supported answers.

6. Accept reasonable and supported answers.

7. Things Sam made include a door, jesses, spear, storage bin, needle, pants, pockets, flour, pancakes, willow whistles, raft, moccasins, etc.

8. Sam puts Frightful on a stump and whistles to get her to come to the meat in his hand. He moves away from her and does this again and again. Then he throws a lure for her to catch and retrieve. He doesn't let her eat the prey she catches.

9. Fireplaces must be properly vented or the fumes can kill you.

10. Bando and Thoreau share the following similarities: they love the outdoors, they enjoy the challenge of making new things, they like living off the land and playing willow whistles, etc.

11. Jesse C. James, The Baron, and Frightful have all befriended Sam. They are all warm-blooded animals who live on the mountain with Sam and keep him company, etc.

12. Accept reasonable and supported answers.

Page 27

Answers may vary.

Page 29

1. For Halloween Sam decides to have a party and feed the wild animals.

2. Sam has mittens, a jacket, pants, and moccasins made of deerskin. He also has fur-lined underwear.

3. Accept reasonable and supported answers.

4. No, the party turns out badly. The animals raid Sam's cache of food, invade his tree, and a skunk sprays him.

5. Sam is lonely after Bando leaves, so he visits town and meets "Mr. Jacket." He's glad to have met someone his own age.

6. No, Sam may have been killed by a bullet from a hunter's gun. In fact, he does come close to getting shot.

Answer Key (cont.)

7. Sam suddenly realizes that he needs a lot of firewood for his fireplace.

8. Accept reasonable and supported answers.

9. People will be curious about him now that he's been seen in town. They may try to look for him.

10. It was harder to tan the deer hide he obtained in the fall because it needed to be soaked in tannic acid in an oak stump. However, the water kept freezing in the stump.

11. Accept reasonable and supported answers.

12. Accept reasonable and supported answers.

Page 32

1. 212 days x 23 walnuts = 4,876 walnuts

2. 14 days + 16 days = 30 days (must start by October 1)

3. 115 x 6 hours = 690 hours

4. 15 x 32 = 480 trees

5. 480 x 95% = 456 trees or 5% x 480 = 24 trees; 480 – 24 = 456 trees

6. 372 x 24 hours in a day = 8,928 hours rounds to 8,930 hours

Page 33

Allow any reasonable responses.

1. scrabbly = scruffy and shabbily

2. stroobly = stubbly and droopy

3. scuttering = scurry and scattering

4. nubby = nub and stubby

5. chittering = chatting and twittering

Page 34

1. Bando and Sam's dad both come to visit him on Christmas.

2. Sam knows that Bando likes the moccasins he made for him from his facial expression and because Bando puts them right on.

3. Things that Sam does during the winter include snowshoeing, sledding, watching the birds, playing his whistle, talking to Frightful, cutting food for the deer, etc.

4. At first Sam's dad is skeptical about Frightful until he finds out how useful she is. Then he keeps complimenting the bird.

5. Sam tells Matt Spell about the wild boy because subconsciously he wants to be found.

6. Sam doesn't have any greens in his winter diet, leaving him lacking in vitamins.

7. One day Sam went to town and met a boy he called "Mr. Jacket" in the pharmacy. Later he learns Tom Sidler is his name.

8. Sam cuts down branches for the starving deer to eat. He does this because they've already eaten everything they could reach.

9. Frightful was following her instincts to find a mate.

10. Accept yes or no answers as long as they're well-supported.

11. No; even Sam realizes that she wouldn't be able to survive in the wild because of how she's been raised.

12. Accept yes or no answers as long as they're well-supported.

Page 37

1. hyperbole; a thousand miles

2. personification; tree moans

3. simile; like

4. hyperbole; eaten in years

5. personification; stream ran, jumped, splashed

6. simile; as

7. personification; boulders guarded

8. verbification; rollercoastering; caterpillaring

9. hyperbole; when the world began

10. simile; like

11. verbification; wormed

12. hyperbole; heart lift my sweater

13. personification; weasel lecture

Page 41

Part I: Matching

1. D emphatic
2. N ravine
3. H berated
4. J savory
5. K tedious
6. B copse
7. I furtively
8. E sanguine
9. C devour
10. G resounding

Part II: True/False

1. False (Sam's first night on his own is scary and frustrating. He can't get a fire started. He builds his lean-to in a windy spot. His hook breaks when he tries to catch fish and then he can't cook the fish he does catch. A whippoorwill keeps him awake.)

2. False (Sam encounters a man named Bill who helps him practice with his flint and steel until he can start a fire.)

3. True

4. False (While under attack by the mother falcon, Sam takes a baby falcon from her nest. She is in good health, and he names her Frightful. Sam eventually trains Frightful to catch food for him.)

Answer Key *(cont.)*

5. True

6. True

7. True

8. False (Sam is resourceful and willing to try eating different things. Sam gets meat by setting traps, fishing, and teaching Frightful to hunt. He digs up wild plants and roots and finds nuts, apples, and berries.)

9. True

10. False (Making the blueberry jam is Bando's idea. Bando makes jam storage pots out of clay and goes to town to get sugar. Then together Sam and Bando figure out how to make the jam through trial-and-error.)

11. False (During the week after Christmas Sam has both his father and Bando living with him.)

12. False (Although the ice storm destroys many trees on the mountain, Sam's tree house is undamaged.)

13. True

14. False (Sam tells Matt Spell what to write in a newspaper article about the wild boy of the Catskills. He gives Matt some facts and some false information.)

15. True

Page 42

1. Sam says that the land is just the place for a Gribley because he is a Gribley, and he is extremely happy living off the land.

2. Amazingly the weasel, whom Sam nicknames The Baron, is not afraid of Sam. Instead, he is so infuriated by having been caught in his trap that when he finally escapes, instead of fleeing, he shows his displeasure by running up Sam's body and making angry noises, which Sam calls a lecture.

3. Sam feels pleased that even though they are lowly creatures, earthworms can create a stir in the world. It makes him wonder if even though he is just one boy living alone on a mountain, he is having an effect on the world, too.

4. Bando, a college professor, felt that his life was interesting until he meets Sam and sees all the things he is doing to survive all by himself on the mountain. Now Bando feels that his life is dull in comparison to Sam's.

5. September blazed a trail into the mountains is Sam's way of saying that autumn was arriving on his mountain. Fall colors are often called blazing colors because they are bright shades of red, orange, and yellow.

6. Sam feels that this is the most real Halloween night he's ever experienced because he is afraid. The Halloween party he meant to have with the animals gets out of control, forcing him to chase the animals away and get sprayed by a skunk in the process.

7. Sam keeps a close eye on the weather and learns to read the clouds and breezes to know when a storm is coming. He learns to do this so that he won't get caught out in a downpour or a blizzard.

8. Sam discovers that when you are hungry your body will often crave the specific type of food that it needs. For example, in midwinter he began craving liver because his body needed vitamins, and he had not eaten any fruits or vegetables for a long time.

9. Sam tells Matt Spell this because a lot of the food that he has eaten on the mountain tastes like spinach and oysters. His diet has relied heavily on area plants, roots, and mussels.

10. In Sam's dream his falcon Frightful tells him that he has behaved in a way that indicates that he actually wants to be found. Sam's subconscious is telling him what he can't admit to himself.

11. Sam is saying that even if you live in a crowded city with lots of people around you, you can still be very lonesome. He feels that some people are actually lonelier than he is because he has Frightful and The Baron to keep him company.

12. Sam means that he can tell his mother loves the mountain and wants to settle down here.

Page 43
Answers will vary. Accept reasonable responses.